3 Beginners Edition
Ebonygeek45

Project 3

Uno Easy Starter Project : LED Cube

Arduino Uno Building and Coding

Shannon Davis

i

ii

DEDICATION

This book is dedicated to those daring enough to try this project. To those who actually want to drill through the code to see how it works. To those with the curiosity to take what they learn further.

Ebonygeek45 aka Shannon Davis

iii

TABLE OF CONTENTS

INTRODUCTION

When you start programming electronics it is like a bug. You are bitten and you keep going. It is fun to see what you can do.

The programming can be frustrating at times. But it is a part of learning and you are always going forward. Sometimes it take putting something away for a while. You may decide to come back to it after a week...a month...a year. At that time you may have work through some problems. Maybe it just take you stepping away, when you come back to it you can work through the problems. The problem may be with the electronics or with the programming. One thing is for sure, when you get it working right you feel like your on top of the world.

Then it is on to the next project.

The led cube is something that I had been looking at for a while. I kept saying that I would get to it later.

When I did get to it I can say it was a joy to work with. Ideas for a bigger and better one is definitely brewing in my head. I will get to that later. That rework on the reverse engineered car is sitting on the back burner. There is also a small robot project that is sitting in my head as well. Then of course the automatic lights in the house.

The joys of working with electronics and programming. Once yours eyes are opened to it you just keep going on.

You start to think different and some of your projects may be completely electronic. Like the windmill set up I want to add to the solar set up I already have.

Also, experimenting with the neodymium powerful magnets to see what I can do with those. That is something I just can't for the world of me remember to order. But I have some ideas for them. Well, maybe when they are more in the budget.

Why am I telling you all this. If you are the sort that love to put together huge jigsaw puzzles. You like to do word puzzles and that type of thing. You like to put things together. Then you may want to get into the world of electronics and programming. There is no better challenge in my opinion.

Each project teach you a bit more about electronics and programming. That is whether you are a pro at it or a hobbyist like me.

The cube is a great project and without further ado....let's jump in.

v

CHAPTER 1: ABOUT THE CUBE

The next project in this series will be building and programming a 4x4x4 led cube.

This is the perfect project for a beginner to get there feet wet so to speak. Don't be intimidated. This is the fun part. Enjoy the process of working through it.

Instead of the one led cube from series 1 and 2 SOS project. This project will have 64 leds. It will use the Arduino Uno(and the usb cord of course). There will be 4 resistors, the cube shield, 2 shift registers, Male headers(short leg and long legged), 2 IC sockets, and wires to connect the negative leads. Don't worry there is a kit that supply all that. You do have to buy the wires if you don't already have them.

This book is adding to what was learned in the first 2 Beginners Editions series books.

Beginners Edition Ebonygeek45 SOS Project 1 Uno Programming digitalWrite.

Beginners Edition Ebonygeek45 SOS Project 2 Uno Programming digitalWrite More on C++.

The only function that has not been been used in project 1 and 2 is the – shiftOut – function.

For the arrays – sizeof – has not been shown in project 1 and 2.

Bits are also something new we will be going over in this book.

Project 1 and 2 did cover Arduino functions digitalWrite and pinMode, and much more not used for this program.

Project 1 and 2 also explained variables, user defined functions, calling functions, passing variables and references to functions, if statements, for loops, arrays, attributes and behaviors, algorithms, comments, and optimizing your code.

If you don't have the first two project books in the series, no worries this book explains the project easily. It is an advantage to have the books because they will help you to understand the basics that are the building blocks to the programming. Not just for this project but for all projects you may be doing. It is strongly suggested to buy the first two books in the series.

In addition you will need a soldering iron and solder.

You want to pay attention to the solder you get to use with your project. 60/40 Rosin core solder(.032 diameter light duty) is what I would suggest. Your not looking for the big plumber solder. It won't work for your electronics. There is a Radio Shack brand I like to use. However I would suggest a different place for the soldering iron.

My first soldering iron that I really like was a Weller Medium Duty 40 Watt soldering Iron. I did a review on it on YouTube.

Weller Solder Iron and MakerShield Kit

https://youtu.be/6LagZVlJY9g

Don't be intimidated by the thought of soldering. If I can do it anyone can. My best advise is to take your time with it. This project is good for beginners because soldering all the leds will give you a good amount of practice. Soldering the components on the shield will further that practice. Developing you soldering skills is a big advantage to prototyping, and dealing with electronics.

My strong suggestion is to use the ICStation 4X4X4 Light Cube Kit for Arduino UNO. The reason I am suggesting this kit is you get all the components included. The kit is a very good price depending on where you get it. I got mine off ebay (free shipping of course). Unfortunately they did not include installation or code documentation. Some vendors do include that information. It is easily found on the ICStation site.

Below is the link for the kit if you don't already have it.

http://www.icstation.com/icstation-4x4x4-light-cube-arduino-p-5312.html?aid=216

This kit is a beginner kit. Once you get this one under your belt, you may want to design your own. I would encourage that you do.

You can try to put together your own version. But, try to keep it inline with the led kit suggested because the code is geared towards this kit. If you go it on your own make sure it is a 4x4x4 cube.

A set of videos on YouTube is available that shows the building process of the ICStation 4X4X4 Light Cube Kit for Arduino UNO.

Led Cube Design Part 1

https://youtu.be/EL-0YjQvM-M

Led Cube Design Part 2

https://youtu.be/-c76-1uXz1I

Led Cube Design Part 3

https://youtu.be/TVDdDVJlGQ0

Led Cube Design Part 4

https://youtu.be/UVH5Na_raUQ

Led Cube Design Part 5

https://youtu.be/bzh0A6CjC3Y

Led Cube Design Part 6

https://youtu.be/B37ByWu2Ksc

You can follow along with the videos or follow along here. I will go into the process quickly. If you get lost anywhere just pull up the videos on YouTube.

About using breadboard as a jig to solder your leds.

It worked well for me on both the cubes I did. But when using the breadboard as shown later, there is a chance you may burn the breadboard, or solder may fall on it. That would be horrible. There are ways around that problem. You can also use a perf board and spread it out the same way. People have also drilled holes in a piece of wood to hold the leds in place. Just wanted to warn you of the danger of damage to the breadboard if you decide to do it like I did. If you want to air on the side of caution google creating a rig for led cube. You should be able to find other ways to hold the leds while soldering.

Let's get to the build.

Pictured here is what you get with the ICStation 4X4X4 Light Cube Kit for Arduino UNO

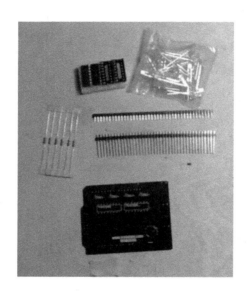

The kit includes:

A bag of leds

resistors(500 ohms) 6

Long foot header pins

Round header pins

16 p ic sockets 2

74HC595 shift registers 2

The cube shield.

There was no documentation with the kit.

But you can't let those things worry you.

It is a good thing to be able to research, and sometimes you learn more.

Again the kit provides you with all you need except for the wires for the cathode lines.

CHAPTER 2: TESTING THE LEDS

First and very important, you need to test each led. Don't skip this step.

Imagine working carefully to get the cube built. Maybe making some mistakes and having to fix them.

Then finding out that one of the leds is not working. Then having to go back and replace it.

It is best to test the leds first to avoid that problem.

It is not hard, just a bit boring. You can go about testing the leds a couple of ways.

One way is using a breadboard to test the Leds.

Connect the ground and positive from your breadboard to your Arduino Uno. Then test them one by one.

Make sure the anode(positive, long leg) is connected to the anode row on the breadboard, and the cathode(negative, short leg) is connected to the cathode row on the breadboard.

A Proto-board is another easy and convenient way to test your Leds.

Just touch the positive and negative leg of the Led to the middle positive and negative strip on the proto-board. It should light up the Led, as long as the Led is good.

It arrive already assembled in most cases.

It is also a shield that fits on top of the Arduino Uno.

If you would like to order the protoboard the link is below.

http://www.icstation.com/prototype-shield-protoshield-mini-breadboard-arduino-duemila-p-2724.html?aid=216

You get some of the best deals from Ebay if that is the route you want to go. Especially when getting the shipping free. But it takes a while for the shipment to arrive. Some of the vendors send something close to but not what's ordered.

For the most part for the money you save. Ebay is a good place to get your electronics (Be careful when ordering from Ebay.).

It would be best to order the Led cube kit through the company that made it. Again the link is:

Below is the link for the kit if you don't already have it.

http://www.icstation.com/icstation-4x4x4-light-cube-arduino-p-5312.html?aid=216

The links being provided to you to order is for your convenience. At this time we have had no problems when ordering from this site. So we are referring you to them. If you do order from this site and you have problems with their products please let us know. We will let others know of the problems as well. Email us at: ebonynerd45@gmail.com and just put problem with cube shield in the subject line.

CHAPTER 3: THE SHIELD

1. Long foot header pins.

These are the headers that will connect the cube to the Arduino. When you get them they will be in a strip.

They will need to be cut(broken apart) according to the shield holes.

2 8 pin sections

2 6 pin sections

On one side of the shield there is 2 8 pin sections. On the other side of the shield there are 2 6 pin sections.

Carefully count out the pins and break them apart.

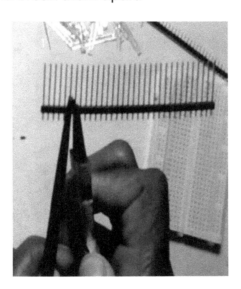

When doing this I use two sets of pliers. It doesn't matter if they are

needle nose or flat head. Just so you can get a good grip on the strip

to break them apart correctly.

Note: Just break them apart then sit them to the side.

The black housing is kept for these.

You will have some spares. Set them to the side because you can use them later.

2. Round header pins – lets just rename them anode pins for now.

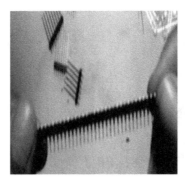

They also come in a strip. The shiny pins inside the black strip is what we want. That means we need to break them out of the black strip.

The wire strippers was good for this. Use the sharp edge that you cut the wires with to cut through the strip pin by pin.

Then cut the black housing off each pin.

Be careful when breaking them out. They tend to go flying across the table sometimes.

Note: If you just want to cut each pin off and leave the surrounding black housing you can do that. It just looks all shiny and nice when you remove it.

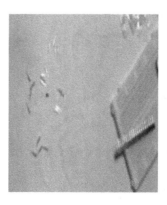

Once you have your anode pins separated, it's time to start soldering.

3. These pins is what we want to solder first.

You will be soldering on the same side as the company information. The layout for the resistors and ic socket is on the soldering side too. On the other side you will see where the pins fit.

You will have in all 20 pins to solder in. That's 16 for the anodes and 4 for the cathodes. D0 through D19.

You could sit all the pins in the shield(make sure that you have them in the right side of the shield). Then use strips of tape to hold them in while you solder the other side.

Here each corner pin was soldered on the shield one at a time.

That way the rest of the pins could be added one at a time without the shield tilting.

Just take your time and be patient however you decide to do it. This is good soldering practice.

Make sure you are not adding to much solder.

If you are a beginner with soldering, practice does make perfect. Make sure to correct mistakes as they happen. Take your time.

This is how it should look once all your pins are soldered in.

It is important to solder these pins in first.

To solder them in later would mean the two that sit under the ic socket would be hard if not impossible to do.

4. Add both your IC Sockets.

Make sure it matches with the outline for the IC Socket.

Make sure the notch on the board matches the notch on the IC Socket. That is very important.

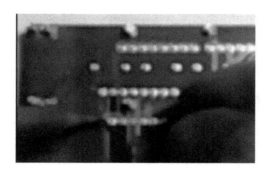

Then you want to flip it over as shown. You are soldering on the opposite side of the shield now.

The best way to do this is to solder a lead on each side of the ic socket for both. That will hold it in securely while you solder the rest of the leads in.

Once the IC socket leads are soldered in. It's time for the resistors.

Bridging:

Make sure that the solder does not melt onto another pin connecting them. That is bridging, which has it's uses sometimes,

On this shield there are no bridges. In the case that you see a bridge when you inspect the shield, it will have to be fixed.

Just drag your soldering iron between the two solder joints.

Inspect your soldering closely to make sure it is soldered the right way.

5. Flip the shield back over then add the resistors. Make sure it matches with the outline for the resistors.

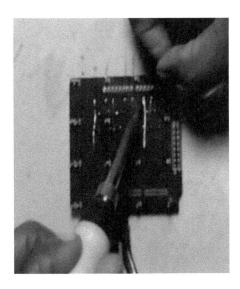

On the other side bend the leads close to the shield. That will hold them in place while you solder them on. You can put them all in at the same time. Just try to bend the leads so they are not in the way of you soldering the other resistors.

Once they are soldered, cut off your leads.

It is a good idea to buy side snips. They are perfect for cutting off leads.

Note: Save the leads for other projects.

6. This is how the shield will look once the resistors and the dip sockets are added. Make sure to line up the curved notch on the IC socket with the outline of it on the shield.

The resistors are not polarized. I just like to line up the colors of the bands in the same direction.

Make sure this is what you have. Go back and correct anything that isn't right if needed.

7. Now it is time for the Long foot header pins. The side with the long legs is set in the side of the shield with the company information on it. Make sure they are on the correct side.

It will be soldered on the same side as the resistors and the IC pin was soldered on. Just like the IC block solder one side then solder the rest of the header pins.

8. Now carefully insert the shift registers into the IC sockets.

Be very careful not to break the legs. Do not bend the legs no more than needed to get them in the socket correctly.

Most of the time with patience they go right in.

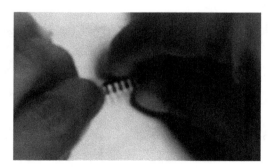

If not, sit the Shift Register on it's side on a hard surface and rock it gently on each side.

You want it to bend just enough to fit into the IC socket.

The legs are easy to bend too much so do this carefully.

Then try easing it into the IC socket.

Make sure the notch on the shift register match with the IC socket, which should match with the shield outline.

For now you are done with the shield. Give your self a pat on the back and have a cookie.

CHAPTER 4: MAKING THE SLICES

Let's face it the leds are the most important part of this project.

How you complete this section is important.

You want your cube to look like a cube. You have to pay attention to make sure it is lined up correctly.

It don't have to be perfect, so don't panic.

There are many ways to solder the leds together. From using a breadboard and headers, to

drilling holes in woodblocks. It is all in what you decide to do.

You can use the extra Long foot headers. You may have to move the headers to hold sections as you go.

But you should have enough to work with your slices.

Break apart the long foot header in two's.

Setting up the pins on the breadboard.

Below is two half size breadboards. You can use full size. The most important point here is the middle rails are taken off for both. The side rails are not being used.

The spacing for the headers shows 4 empty holes between headers across. 7 empty holes between headers going down.

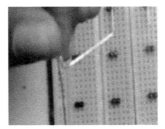

The positive leg of the led is going to be kept straight. The negative leg is bent up. Try to bend them at the same point.

There was an indentation on the leg towards the top. I bent them at that point.

Once you bend them you want to sit the led in the headers. The positive one closest to the breadboard. Position it so the negative is facing the side and meeting with the negative of the next led.

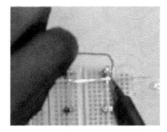

Once you have the first row positioned it's time to solder. Remember again be careful. It don't take a lot of heat to heat up the leads.

You don't want to use so much solder it drips into your breadboard. Or worse you don't want to burn the breadboard.

Solder the negative leads across. For your first row of 4 leds.

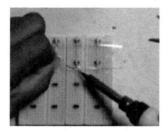

Now, we are down to the second row. The difference is that we have to solder the positive leads, as well as the negatives.

My process was to solder the positive first, Then on to the negative. Make sure they are spaced correctly.

The positive leg should also meet with the positive leg of the led below it.

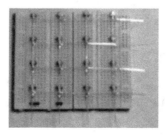

Keep going until the 4 rows are soldered for the negatives and positive leads.

Once your first slice is done, you have three more to go. Carefully remove the first slice from the headers.

Do the 2nd, 3rd and 4th the same way.

When you have all 4 slices done, it is almost complete.

CHAPTER 5: CONNECTING THE SLICES TO THE SHIELD

Carefully insert the anode leads into the shield. At this point the shield should be inserted into the Uno.

The negative leads of the slices need to be on the same side as the cathode row on the shield. Which is

D16, D17, D18, and D19.

Insert all four slices.

In order to keep the slices from being pulled out by mistake, the leads for this cube was soldered to the headers on the shield. You may choose to do the same, or not.

The last part is dealing with the cathode rows.

This part will involve using wire to run down to the cathode headers. The best wire to use is 22 AWG hook up wire.

Also, solid would be best. But, if you do use stranded you need to solder on a lead so it will go into the negative header pins.

You can bend the negative lead to the side and solder it to the negative lead across from it.

Once all 4 leads are soldered You would solder your wire to it. That wire would run down and be inserted into the cathode header.

Each row connect to a negative header pin.

The lowest level of the cube(lets say section 1) wire connects to D16.

Next row section 2 wire connects to D17.

Next row section 3 wire connects to D18.

The top row section 4 wire connects to D19.

Once you are done you led cube is finished. That is the hardware part of it.

For someone with more experience the shield is not needed. They would be able to figure out how to wire the shift registers, resistors, and the headers to the cube. Then pin it out to the Arduino. It will involve more soldering and wires.

But for a beginner this kit is a very good way to learn how it all works. Then you can step up to doing a cube without the shield.

The kit however is a very good value considering that all the components come with it.

Some key things to remember while constructing you cube is:

Neatness is the name of the game here. The more uniform you get it, the better your cube will look during your light shows.

Warning: When using the breadboard to set up what we call the slices...Be careful not to burn or drop solder on the breadboard.

Make sure that you measure out the spaces evenly and consistently. You want to be able to solder easily, You also want it to be spaced out in squares nicely.

Make sure you bend the leads neatly and that anodes are not touching cathodes.

Anodes are the positive leads(longer leg) and cathodes are the negative leads(shorter leg).

Take your time and enjoy the process.

CHAPTER 6: STEPPING UP YOUR IDE?

Now for the coding.

You can use the Arduino IDE.

At this point you may choose to step up to a more interactive IDE. It may take a little bit of set up, but there are some big advantages

Eclipse has a pretty good IDE with all the bells and whistles. It is very useful with features like:

- Auto Completion
- Refactoring
- All kinds of short cut keys.
- Hovering over functions to review them.
- Syntax Highlighting
- Many many more features

The biggest advantage is ease of reviewing functions by hovering over the name of the function.

When you step up your IDE you can really start working with your code in style.

Eclipse is very popular for their Arduino plugin. The most recent version is Eclipse Neon. This plug in was easier to set up then others. But getting it set up may be tricky. The older versions work better than the new in some cases.

You can view the setup process on YouTube where it is walked through for Eclipse Neon.

Just look it up on my channel ebonygeek45.

Codeblock also offer support for Arduino coding. It looks promising. They seem to be trying to develop a graphical interface too.

There are many more, I can't speak for the others. I have not used them all that much.

There is more support out there now for coding and convenience than when I started. It is getting easier to set up the coding environment with interactive IDE's. It allow the coding to be more fun and easier to track down problems.

If you find it too difficult to set up another IDE, the Arduino IDE works in a pinch..

CHAPTER 7: PLOTTING OUT YOUR PROGRAM

The shift register is the driving force to the cube. Since it is the brains it just make sense to know a little about it. It is an IC chip.

IC means Integrated circuit.

This means that it is a circuit packaged up in a little chip. A cube can be made without the shift register. Just like the shield we are using the shift register makes the cube more streamlined without the need for more wiring and components.

When dealing with IC's you want to know what circuits are involved in the chip. For that you would look up the data sheet. Most of the time when you order an IC it doesn't come with one. If you know the name of the chip It is as simple as googling it.

We know the name of the IC that comes with this kit is the 74HC595.

Google 74HC595 datasheet and you will see many datasheets come up.

Arduino ShiftOut will come up under the results. This is good because there may be a function provided that can be used. Although it is not giving an example of the cube it is giving an example of how to connect with the shift register. It also gives a pinout diagram for the shift register.

Working from that you see that you will need three things to use this function. The datapin, clockpin and latchpin.

If you take a look at the code sample 1.1 Hello World at:

https://www.arduino.cc/en/Tutorial/ShftOut11

It gives you an idea of what you can do with the function.

This can work for us.

Taking a look at that code;

```
******************************************************

#include "Arduino.h"


//****************************************************************//

//Name: shiftOutCode, Hello World
//Author : Carlyn Maw,Tom Igoe, David A. Mellis
//Date: 25 Oct, 2006
//Modified: 23 Mar 2010
```

//Version : 2.0

// Notes   : Code for using a 74HC595 Shift Register to count from 0 to 255

//***

//Pin connected to ST_CP of 74HC595

```
int latchPin = 8;
```

//Pin connected to SH_CP of 74HC595

```
int clockPin = 12;
```

////Pin connected to DS of 74HC595

```
int dataPin = 11;
```

```
void setup() {
//set pins to output so you can control the shift register

        pinMode(latchPin, OUTPUT);
        pinMode(clockPin, OUTPUT);
        pinMode(dataPin, OUTPUT);
}
```

```
void loop() {
// count from 0 to 255 and display the number
// on the LEDs
        for (int numberToDisplay = 0; numberToDisplay < 256; numberToDisplay++)
        {
                // take the latchPin low so
                // the LEDs don't change while you're sending in bits:
                digitalWrite(latchPin, LOW);
                // shift out the bits:
                shiftOut(dataPin, clockPin, MSBFIRST, numberToDisplay);

                //take the latch pin high so the LEDs will light up:
                digitalWrite(latchPin, HIGH);
                // pause before next value:
                delay(500);
        }
}
```

****

The above code is for references. It is not a part of the cube code.

This gives us an idea of what we need to do.

The above code shows the setting up of variables to the dataPin, clockPin and latchPin. The dataPin and ClockPin is to be used in the shiftOut function. The latchpin is to be used with the digitalwrite function.

The comments is of course explaining why. Always pay attention to the comments.

Of course you can make your own function, but using the shiftOut function helps with the busy work. It also gives us our start. for the program.

Don't forget to take a look at the shift register's datasheet. The pinout of the chip is;

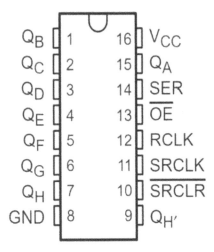

Pin 15 is QA then over to pins 1 - 7 which is QB - QH. These are your outputs for the shift register. There are 8 for each shift register. This is important to note. Since we have two shift registers on the shield that mean there will be 16 outputs.

On the shield D0 through D15 is the anode pins. That is 16. The anode pins are wired to the 16 outputs on the shift registered. Or in the case of the shield, the anode pins are traced to the outputs of the shift register.

Pin 8 GND is the ground for the shift register.

Hopping over to Pin 16 which is VCC. It is the positive for the shift register. VCC and ground supplies power to the shift registers.

The pins left over is pins 9 through Pin 14. That is 6 pins. These pins are specifically for shifting the data to light the leds

Pin 9 shows as QH', with the quote after it(Don't confuse that with pin 7 QH). They are different. This is the Serial Out Pin. This pin is used when you have more than one shift register. We have two. In other words this pin shifts data to another shift register. You can add as many shift registers as you need for a project.

Considering the function that we are using, We know there are 3 pins it will program. The datapin, clockpin and latchpin.

The datapin is pin14 SER, clockpin is pin 11, and the latchpin is pin 12.

That leaves 2 pins that we will not code on the shift register. Those 2 are pin 10 SRCLR, and Pin 13 OE

Getting back to the program for the cube.

I am going to work from an algorithm. Taking it through that process will cause less problems. The cube algorithm is below.

The cube algorithm

1.

First we will deal with setting up the shift register.

2.

Set up the negative array.(Cathodes on shield)

3.

Set up the positive array.(Anodes on shield)

4.

Create and write the program for the shift register.

5.

Create and write the program

for the cathode array and speed of flashing.

6.

Create and write the program for

the anode patterns and updates.

7.

       Create patterns to run on the cube in the anode array.

8.

Send it all to the loop.

9.

Do the final verify and test.

10.

Troubleshoot and document any problems and how they were solved.

11.

Treat yourself to a slice of strawberry shortcake.

The algorithm is so that you keep on track for what you are doing. It is a way to keep your programming on track and not get lost in it. But don't be afraid to change it up if what you are trying is not working. Just make sure to add what did work to it for future references.

It takes patience and time to work out a good program.

Seek out forums for when you get stuck.

There is no shame in finding code that matches what you want to do through google. Then adjusting it to what you want. This in a way is a shortcut.

But it also helps you learn how to work with code. As well as how to read the code.

It helps your programming to actually dig down into the code that you may find. Find out how it work and customize it to what you want.

Don't just copy it and paste it, then settle for if it work or kind of work.

Look into the functions, test out ways to make the code do exactly what you want it to do. Study why the author of code you may have found did what he did, then try to improve it.

In that way you will begin to learn how to do your own functions and program. As you get better you will be able to program your own programs quickly and easily.

CHAPTER 8: STARTING WITH SHIFT REGISTER CODE

Putting on that coding and thinking cap, and we are ready.. The variables and set up function we are going to need is below.

Starting off a fresh sketch.

File > New

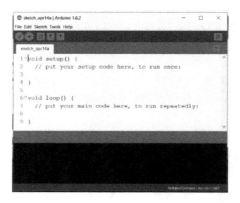

Save the sketch to the name you want. Make the name descriptive so you know what it is for.

Ie LedCube.

File > Save As > Delete what is in File Name and add the name you want. Ie LedCube > Click Save.

Now we can start adding code to the new sketch. The includes, variables and arrays are going to be added above the setup function. The new functions we are making(User defined functions) are going to be added between the setup and loop function.

You are starting with:

```
*******************************************************
```

// LedCube

// put your includes here

// put your variables here

// put your arrays here

void setup()

{

// put your setup code here, to run once:

```
}
```

// put your functions here

```
void loop()
{
```

// put your main code here, to run repeatedly:

```
}
```

****

Add the Arduino include at the start of your sketch. It is just a good habit to get used to even when using the Arduino IDE.

We will start with the first set of variables. They should be set up below the includes as stated before.

Declare the shift register variables

The sketch starts out:

****

```
// LedCube
// put your includes here
#include "Arduino.h"

// put your variables here
/* Adding serial register variables */
int srClockPin=0;   // Pin connected to Pin 11 of 74HC595 (Clock SHCP)
int srLatchPin=1;   // Pin connected to Pin 12 of 74HC595 (Latch STCP)
int srDataPin=3;    // Pin connected to Pin 14 of 74HC595 (Data DS)

// put your arrays here

void setup()
{
// put your setup code here, to run once:

}
```

// put your functions here

void loop()

{

// put your main code here, to run repeatedly:

}

****

Verify then run your code. There should be no errors at this point.

That is simple because it is the same as the Hello World example we have for shiftOut above.

In setup function

Set the shift register pins to output.

****

// LedCube

// put your includes here

#include "Arduino.h"

// put your variables here

int srClockPin=0;   // Pin connected to Pin 11 of 74HC595 (Clock SHCP)

int srLatchPin=1;   // Pin connected to Pin 12 of 74HC595 (Latch STCP)

int srDataPin=3;   // Pin connected to Pin 14 of 74HC595 (Data DS)

// put your arrays here

void setup()

{

// put your setup code here, to run once:

/* Adding shift register's OUTPUT in pinMode */

```
       pinMode(srClockPin, OUTPUT);
       pinMode(srLatchPin, OUTPUT);
       pinMode(srDataPin, OUTPUT);
```

}

// put your functions here

```
void loop()
{
// put your main code here, to run repeatedly:


}
```

****

Verify then run your code. There should be no errors at this point.

What is this doing? You ask.

We are setting up the pins that the shift register will connect to. The comments is showing the pins on the shift register itself. Remember we are using a shield. The shield is connecting those pins to pins on the Arduino.

Remember we are taking example from the shiftOut program we found when researching the shift register for the coding.

We are building the program for the cube out. Follow along below.

On the shield there is four pins for the negative connections. The pins on the shield are:

D16, D17, D18, and D19.

Here you would want to think out how to deal with the pins that you have.

Go back up to where we added the variables for the shift register. Below that we want to add variables for the cathodes on the shield.

```
/* Cathode variables to be used in Cathode array */
int ledPin16= 4;        // Row 1
int ledPin17= 5;        // Row 2
int ledPin18= 6;        // Row 3
int ledPin19= 7;        // Row 4
```

Let's go back down in the setup function and add those variables for "OUTPUT underneath the code already there for the shift register. We will add:

```
// Setting cathodes to OUTPUT
pinMode(ledPin16, OUTPUT);
pinMode(ledPin17, OUTPUT);
pinMode(ledPin18, OUTPUT);
pinMode(ledPin19, OUTPUT);
```

You should now have:

****

```
// LedCube

// put your includes here

#include <Arduino.h>

// put your variables here

/* Shift Register variables */

int srClockPin=0;   // Pin connected to Pin 11 of 74HC595 (Clock SHCP)

int srLatchPin=1;   // Pin connected to Pin 12 of 74HC595 (Latch STCP)

int srDataPin=3;    // Pin connected to Pin 14 of 74HC595 (Data DS)

/* Adding cathode variables to be used in Cathode array */

int ledPin16= 4;

int ledPin17= 5;

int ledPin18= 6;

int ledPin19= 7;

// put your arrays here

void setup()

{
        // put your setup code here, to run once:
        pinMode(srClockPin, OUTPUT);
        pinMode(srLatchPin, OUTPUT);
        pinMode(srDataPin, OUTPUT);

        /* Adding cathodes to OUTPUT of pinMode */
        pinMode(ledPin16, OUTPUT);
        pinMode(ledPin17, OUTPUT);
        pinMode(ledPin18, OUTPUT);
        pinMode(ledPin19, OUTPUT);
}

// put your functions here

void loop()

{

}
```

****

Verify then run your code. There should be no errors at this point.

Go back up to where you added the variables for the cathodes.

Below it we are going to add an array. Using an array is a very simple way of working with the negative and positive values for the cube. Arrays are useful in general when coding. They can be a bit tricky, but they are worth learning to use in the long run.

Arrays and variables allow for the optimization of your code. You can program without them, but that would lead to a lot of repeating code. As well as more chances for errors.

The array that we are going to setup using the cathode variables is type int and named negativePins, It is shown below.

int negativePins[] = { <variables> };

Adding the variables for the cathode pins and we now have the completed array for the cathodes.

int negativePins[] = {ledPin16, ledPin17, ledPin18, ledPin19};

Arrays are explained in detail the 2nd edition book in this series.

Note: The arrays need to be the same type. Both negative(cathode) and positive(anodes) would be ints. We want it to be the same kind of data. That would mean negative(cathode) is one type of data and positive(anodes)is another type of data. Each data type is handled differently.

The sketch so far should be:

```
********************************************************

// LedCube

// put your includes here

#include <Arduino.h>

// put your variables here

/* Shift Register variables */

int srClockPin=0;   // Pin connected to Pin 11 of 74HC595 (Clock SHCP)

int srLatchPin=1;   // Pin connected to Pin 12 of 74HC595 (Latch STCP)

int srDataPin=3;    // Pin connected to Pin 14 of 74HC595 (Data DS)

/* Cathode variables to be used in Cathode array */

int ledPin16= 4;

int ledPin17= 5;

int ledPin18= 6;
```

```
int ledPin19= 7;

// put your arrays here
/* Adding cathode variable array */
int negativePins[] = {ledPin16, ledPin17, ledPin18, ledPin19};

void setup()
{
        // put your setup code here, to run once:
        pinMode(srClockPin, OUTPUT);
        pinMode(srLatchPin, OUTPUT);
        pinMode(srDataPin, OUTPUT);

        // Setting cathodes to OUTPUT
        pinMode(ledPin16, OUTPUT);
        pinMode(ledPin17, OUTPUT);
        pinMode(ledPin18, OUTPUT);
        pinMode(ledPin19, OUTPUT);
}
// put your functions here

void loop()
{
}
```

****

Verify then run your code. There should be no errors at this point.

So far so good. Our next step is to set up the positive array.(Anodes on shield)

we are going back to the top and below the Cathode Array:

We need an anode array for the management of the very important bits we will be using.

The two shift registers that come with the kit are 8 bits.

D0 through D7(On the cube shield) are controlled through shift register one for the first 2 rows of the cube.

D8 through D15(On the cube shield) are controlled through shift register two for the second 2 rows of the cube.

This array control's the whole cube.

A little about binary:

Bits are the smallest units of memory you can use. There are 8 bits in a byte. Bits store either 0 or 1 as there value only.

This works well with the Arduino since low is 0 and high is 1. Also, because there is limited memory in the Arduino Uno.

There are 256 combinations possible using 8 bits.

This is very useful when programming colors for RGB leds(not used here.). You may have seen that code. That is if you have researched using bits. But don't confuse it with how it is being used now.

Later we will show how to set up certain patterns using very simple combinations.

Here we are setting up the array for both shift registers. The 8 bit combination is set to 0. So all the leds are off.

We create the array

// Anode Array

unsigned char anodePins[] = {

};

Now to add the bit code for the patterns. Set to the 0 value for now.

// Anode Array

unsigned char anodePins[] = {

B00000000, B00000000, B00000000, B00000000, B00000000, B00000000, B00000000, B00000000,

};

The sketch at this point should be:

****

// LedCube

// put your includes here

#include <Arduino.h>

// put your variables here

/* Shift Register variables */

int srClockPin=0; // Pin connected to Pin 11 of 74HC595 (Clock SHCP)

```
int srLatchPin=1;   // Pin connected to Pin 12 of 74HC595 (Latch STCP)

int srDataPin=3;    // Pin connected to Pin 14 of 74HC595 (Data DS)

/* Cathode variables to be used in Cathode array */

int ledPin16= 4;

int ledPin17= 5;

int ledPin18= 6;

int ledPin19= 7;


// put your arrays here

int negativePins[] = {ledPin16, ledPin17, ledPin18, ledPin19};

/* Adding anodePins array. */

unsigned char anodePins[] = {

// The shift register's outputs is connected to the anodes. There are 2 shift registers.

B00000000, B00000000, B00000000, B00000000, B00000000, B00000000, B00000000, B00000000,

};

void setup()

{

        // put your setup code here, to run once:
        pinMode(srClockPin, OUTPUT);
        pinMode(srLatchPin, OUTPUT);
        pinMode(srDataPin, OUTPUT);

        // Setting cathodes to OUTPUT
        pinMode(ledPin16, OUTPUT);
        pinMode(ledPin17, OUTPUT);
        pinMode(ledPin18, OUTPUT);
        pinMode(ledPin19, OUTPUT);

}

// put your functions here

void loop()

{

}
```

****

Verify then run your code. There should be no errors at this point.

Creation of the write program for the shift register.

This is going to be simple passing a variable into a function.

This will allow the 8 bits of data from the shift register to be shifted into the array.

This function starts by sending the latch to low. The latch pin is Pin 12 of 74HC595 (Latch STCP). You may see it on schematics as RCLK.

Think of it as:

Opening the latch to let the bits in when you set it low(latch pin).

```
        digitalWrite(srLatchPin, LOW);
```
Then your 8 bits can be shifted in.

This is done with Pin 11 of 74HC595 (Clock SHCP). Schematics may show it as SRCLOCK pin.

shiftOut(srDataPin, srClockPin, LSBFIRST, hc595Value); // Serial Register 1

shiftOut(srDataPin, srClockPin, LSBFIRST, (hc595Value >> 8)); // Serial Register 2

The 8 bits is from the anodePins array.

Then closing the latch when all the bits are in, when you set it high(latch pin).

```
        digitalWrite(srLatchPin, HIGH);
```
The latch pin allows you to shift bits in without the bits showing as they are shifted in.

Note that:

The shiftOut function allows the 8 bits to be shifted in sequence.

The shield has connected the two shift registers together as they are designed to do.

Take note of the last arguments it's parameters.

```
        /* Shifting 8 bits of information per shift register into array */
        shiftOut(srDataPin, srClockPin, LSBFIRST, hc595Value)
        and
        shiftOut(srDataPin, srClockPin, LSBFIRST, (hc595Value >> 8))
```
The functions is:

void write74HC595(unsigned int hc595Value)

```
{

        digitalWrite(srLatchPin, LOW); // Ensures LEDS don't light whilst changing values
        shiftOut(srDataPin, srClockPin, LSBFIRST, hc595Value);
        shiftOut(srDataPin, srClockPin, LSBFIRST, (hc595Value >> 8));
```

```
        digitalWrite(srLatchPin, HIGH);
}
```

Shift out is shown above - shiftOut() - is freebie Arduino code. It is already set up for you to use.

The shift out function takes 4 arguments.

```
        shiftOut(uint8_t dataPin, uint8_t clockPin, uint8_t bitOrder, uint8_t val)
```
in layman's terms.

```
        shiftOut(dataPin, clockPin, bitOrder, data to shift out as value)
```

At this stage the sketch should be:

```
********************************************************
```

```
// LedCube

// put your includes here
#include <Arduino.h>

// put your variables here
/* Shift Register variables */
int srClockPin=0;   // Pin connected to Pin 11 of 74HC595 (Clock SHCP)
int srLatchPin=1;   // Pin connected to Pin 12 of 74HC595 (Latch STCP)
int srDataPin=3;    // Pin connected to Pin 14 of 74HC595 (Data DS)
/* Cathode variables to be used in Cathode array */
int ledPin16= 4;
int ledPin17= 5;
int ledPin18= 6;
int ledPin19= 7;

// put your arrays here
int negativePins[] = {ledPin16, ledPin17, ledPin18, ledPin19};
unsigned char anodePins[] = {
// The shift register's outputs is connected to the anodes. There are 2 shift registers.
B00000000, B00000000, B00000000, B00000000, B00000000, B00000000, B00000000, B00000000,
};
```

```
void setup()

{

        // put your setup code here, to run once:
        pinMode(srClockPin, OUTPUT);
        pinMode(srLatchPin, OUTPUT);
        pinMode(srDataPin, OUTPUT);

        // Setting cathodes to OUTPUT
        pinMode(ledPin16, OUTPUT);
        pinMode(ledPin17, OUTPUT);
        pinMode(ledPin18, OUTPUT);
        pinMode(ledPin19, OUTPUT);

}

// put your functions here

/* Adding write74HC595 function.

Shifting 8 bits of information per shift register into array */

void write74HC595(unsigned int hc595Value)

{

        digitalWrite(srLatchPin, LOW);
        shiftOut(srDataPin, srClockPin, LSBFIRST, hc595Value);
        shiftOut(srDataPin, srClockPin, LSBFIRST, (hc595Value >> 8));
        digitalWrite(srLatchPin, HIGH);

}

void loop()

{

}
```

****

Verify then run your code. There should be no errors at this point.

This is necessary for the shift registers to do their work. Shift registers are handy little ic's and can be used for many different components. They are very good for when you need more output pins than your micro-controller supply.

Next step. Create and write the program for the cathode array and speed of flashing.

The function to create is::

void display (unsigned int *anodePins)

This is simple passing a variable into a function.

Here is where we configure the cathodes used in the array we set up.

The anodePins array is being passed to the display function.

It is used later in the if statement within this-function.

The display function is using for loops and if statements.

Study the code until you can understand it.

These concepts are explained in detail in the first 2 books in this series.

To explain it used here:

The display(unsigned int *anodePins) function starts with a for loop.

```
        for (int i=0; i<4; i++){ }
```
The conditions of the for loop is; as long as i is less that 4 add one by increment. The count starts at 0.

When it get to 3 that will be the 4 count. Each time the conditions are true, the loop will run it's instructions.

The instructions in it's loop happens to be another for loop. This second for loop is nested because it is inside another for loop.

```
for (int i=0; i<4; i++)

{

        for (int g=0; g<800; g++)
        {

        }
}
```

How a nested for loop work:

The original for loop evaluate to true. It runs it's instructions. The instructions is the second for loop.

As long as the 2nd for loop is true it will run the instructions in it's loop. Once it evaluate to false, it will break out of this second loop and into the original loop. If the conditions in the original loop is still true it will run the second for loop from the beginning. When the second for loop evaluate to false it will break out of it's loop again.

This will happen as long as the original for loop is true. When the original for loop evaluate to false it will break out of it's loop and the program will continue on.

There are times when this is good like for this function.

It is good for anything where you need to cycle through code. This is a good example to show

```
        pinMode(ledPin16, OUTPUT);
        pinMode(ledPin17, OUTPUT);
        pinMode(ledPin18, OUTPUT);
        pinMode(ledPin19, OUTPUT);
}

// put your functions here

/* Shifting 8 bits of information per shift register into array */

void write74HC595(unsigned int hc595Value)

{

        digitalWrite(srLatchPin, LOW);
        shiftOut(srDataPin, srClockPin, LSBFIRST, hc595Value);
        shiftOut(srDataPin, srClockPin, LSBFIRST, (hc595Value >> 8));
        digitalWrite(srLatchPin, HIGH);
}

/* Adding display(unsigned int *anodePins) function */

void display(unsigned int *anodePins)

{

        for (int i=0; i<4; i++)
        {
                for (int g=0; g<800; g++)
                {
                        if (g==0)
                        {
                                digitalWrite(negativePins[0], HIGH);
                                digitalWrite(negativePins[1], HIGH);
                                digitalWrite(negativePins[2], HIGH);
                                digitalWrite(negativePins[3], HIGH);
                                // Adding the values for the leds
                                write74HC595(anodePins[i]);
                                digitalWrite(negativePins[i], LOW);
                        }
                }
        }
}

void loop()

{

}
```

****

Verify then run your code. There should be no errors at this point.

The next set of variables added are going to be placed under the arrays over the setup function. The main reason for this is because the variable numPatterns make use of the anodePins array. Because the compiler reads code from top to bottom the anodePins array need to be defined so numPatterns can work properly.

These are attributes(supporting variables) to be used in your user defined function behavior displayPattern():

int patternNumber=0;

Used in for loop to configure. Also used in currentPattern array in for loop of if statement using the pattern anodePins array.

int numPatterns=**sizeof**(anodePins)/8;
Used in for loop within if statement to set patternNumber back to 0 once the increment is greater than or equal to pattern number. Using sizeof allows the array to adjust it's size if needed without you doing it.

int tickCount=0;

Used to set up the initial value of tickCount.

int tickCountMax=50;

Used to show how many times to loop before changing the pattern of the cube.

unsigned int currentPattern[4];

Stores and configures the indexes of array anodePins,

The variable tickCount is declared and defined with the other variables in the variable block at the top of the sketch.

The first instructions we have for this function is tickCount-- . That means to decrement by one.

```
void displayPattern()

{
        // only update it every tick otherwise just display as is
        tickCount--;
}
```

The variable tickCount up to this point is 0. To decrement it by one makes it -1.

The if statement after tickCount has the condition of:

If tickCount is less than or equal to 0 it will evaluate to true.

```
void displayPattern()

{

// only update it every tick otherwise just display as is

        tickCount--;

        if (tickCount <= 0)
        {

        }
}
```

Because of the decrement before the if statement it will be true. The instructions for the if statement assigns tickCount a value that is set in tickCountMax 0f 50.

```
void displayPattern()

{

// only update it every tick otherwise just display as is

        tickCount--;
        if (tickCount <= 0)
        {
                tickCount = tickCountMax;
        }
}
```

The next instruction within the if statement is a for loop.

The for loop conditions are i set to 0 to start, if i is less than 4 increment i.

This means the loop will repeat 4 times before the code breaks out of this for loop.

```
void displayPattern()

{

// only update it every tick otherwise just display as is

        tickCount--;
        if (tickCount <= 0)
        {
                tickCount = tickCountMax;
                for (int i=0; i<4; i++)
                {

                }
        }
}
```

The instructions it will repeat as long as it's conditions are true is:

currentPattern[i] = anodePins[i*2 + patternNumber*8] * 256 + anodePins[i*2 + 1 + patternNumber*8];

This is assigning the currentPattern the value of:

anodePins[i*2 + patternNumber*8] * 256

+

anodePins[i*2 + 1 + patternNumber*8]

That is the only directions for this for loop.

When it do break out of the for loop it continues to the next line of code.

```
void displayPattern()

{

// only update it every tick otherwise just display as is

        tickCount--;
        if (tickCount <= 0)
        {
                tickCount = tickCountMax;
                for (int i=0; i<4; i++)
                {
                        // The below code is all one line, not the two showing here
                        currentPattern[i] = anodePins[i*2 + patternNumber*8] * 256 +
                        anodePins[i*2 + 1 + patternNumber*8];
                }
                patternNumber++;
        }
}
```

This sets patternNumber to 1 because it increments up from it's original value of 0 defined when it's variable was declared.

The code continues on to another if statement. It's conditions are patternNumber greater than or equal to numPatterns.

If it evaluates to true we will then go into it's if statement.

```
void displayPattern()

{

// only update it every tick otherwise just display as is

        tickCount--;
        if (tickCount <= 0)
```

```
        {
                tickCount = tickCountMax;
                for (int i=0; i<4; i++)
                {
                        currentPattern[i] = anodePins[i*2 + patternNumber*8] * 256 +
                        anodePins[i*2 + 1 + patternNumber*8];
                }
                patternNumber++;
                if (patternNumber >= numPatterns)
                {
                        patternNumber = 0
                }
        }
}
```

The instructions for this if statement is simply to set

patternNumber to the value of 0 then it breaks out of the

if statement. At that point it breaks out of the for loop.

The next line of code is:

display(&currentPattern[0]);

This is the function call that sends control of the program to that function.

The sketch at this point should be:

****

```
// LedCube
// put your includes here
#include <Arduino.h>

// put your variables here
/* Shift Register variables */
int srClockPin=0;   // Pin connected to Pin 11 of 74HC595 (Clock SHCP)
int srLatchPin=1;   // Pin connected to Pin 12 of 74HC595 (Latch STCP)
int srDataPin=3;    // Pin connected to Pin 14 of 74HC595 (Data DS)
/* Cathode variables to be used in Cathode array */
int ledPin16= 4;
int ledPin17= 5;
```

```
int ledPin18= 6;
int ledPin19= 7;

// put your arrays here
int negativePins[] = {ledPin16, ledPin17, ledPin18, ledPin19};
unsigned char anodePins[] = {
// The shift register's outputs is connected to the anodes. There are 2 shift registers.
B00000000, B00000000, B00000000, B00000000, B00000000, B00000000, B00000000, B00000000,
};

/* Adding Supporting variables(attributes) */
// Put your supporting variables(attributes) here
int patternNumber=0;
int numPatterns=sizeof(anodePins)/8;
int tickCount=0;
int tickCountMax=50;
unsigned int currentPattern[4];

void setup()
{
        // put your setup code here, to run once:
        pinMode(srClockPin, OUTPUT);
        pinMode(srLatchPin, OUTPUT);
        pinMode(srDataPin, OUTPUT);

        // Setting cathodes to OUTPUT
        pinMode(ledPin16, OUTPUT);
        pinMode(ledPin17, OUTPUT);
        pinMode(ledPin18, OUTPUT);
        pinMode(ledPin19, OUTPUT);
}

// put your functions here
/* Shifting 8 bits of information per shift register into array */
void write74HC595(unsigned int hc595Value)
{
```

```
        digitalWrite(srLatchPin, LOW); // Ensures LEDS don't light whilst changing values
        shiftOut(srDataPin, srClockPin, LSBFIRST, hc595Value);
        shiftOut(srDataPin, srClockPin, LSBFIRST, (hc595Value >> 8));
        digitalWrite(srLatchPin, HIGH);
}
void display(unsigned int *anodePins)
{

        for (int i=0; i<4; i++)
        {
                for (int g=0; g<800; g++)
                {
                        if (g==0)
                        {
                                digitalWrite(negativePins[0], HIGH);
                                digitalWrite(negativePins[1], HIGH);
                                digitalWrite(negativePins[2], HIGH);
                                digitalWrite(negativePins[3], HIGH);
                                // Adding the values for the leds
                                write74HC595(anodePins[i]);
                                digitalWrite(negativePins[i], LOW);
                        }
                }
        }
}


/* Adding displayPattern() function. */

void displayPattern()

{

// only update it every tick otherwise just display as is
        tickCount--;
        if (tickCount <= 0)
        {
                tickCount = tickCountMax;
                for (int i=0; i<4; i++)
                {
                        currentPattern[i] = anodePins[i*2 + patternNumber*8] * 256 +
                        anodePins[i*2 + 1 + patternNumber*8];
                }
                patternNumber++;
                if (patternNumber >= numPatterns)
                {
```

```
                    patternNumber = 0;
            }
    }
        display(&currentPattern[0]);
}
void loop()
{
}
```

****

Verify then run your code. There should be no errors at this point.

The " sizeof " concerning the array as shown here optimizes your code. It allows the program to adjust the size of the array. You avoid errors and headaches by setting it up like this. Your array can adjust on it's own according to the array size.

This function deals with timing and updating of the display. It is an interesting function using loops and if statements. The beginner should really study it until they understand the flow. Loops and if statements allow you to create really exciting programs. Any chance you get to pick a function using them apart to see how it works is to your advantage.

Next:

We will also add a call in loop function to the function we just completed.

In this way the code is set up nicely to run.

```
        void loop()
        {
        // put your main code here, to run repeatedly:
                displayPattern();
        }
```

In a way you can think about it as the function calls are footprints.

You know like in the sand.

The program will follow the footprints(function calls)

When I was first leaning C++ I wanted a way to visualize the programs.

My person making the footprints was a pirate. In this case the loop is the start

of the treasure map. The function call or calls in the loop is the footprints.

The best optimization is to only have one function call in the loop.

The function call(footprint) takes you to the first function.

For each function the pirate leaves instructions for you to follow(more footprints).

If there is a for loop or if statement, that is more footprints.

In the case of the for loop you have to do it until the conditions are met. In the case of the if statement you only have to do it if the conditions of the if statement is true.

Once you follow the instructions for the if statement and for loops you are right back where you was in the function. You would follow the next set of instructions after the closing bracket of the if statement or for loop you just ran through. You then continue to follow the instructions(footprints) in that function.

If there is a function call(footprints) at the end of that function you are in, you will be taken to

the next function. Again you follow the instructions of that function, and on and on.

Finally you get to the last function where there is no call to another function. The footprints have come to an end. X mark the spot.

At that point control of the program goes back to our loop function.

Our loop function will repeat the code over and over. The digging for the treasure part of this way of thinking.

If you plotted your map, algorithm, program. However you want to think about it, your program will run. That is the treasure at the end of my pirates map.

OK that may seem a little crazy but it worked for me and a few kids I was explaining C++ to.

For the sci-fi more technical person, you can think of the function call as teleportation instead of footprints. Whatever makes your visualization of the program easiest.

The more adult way of thinking about it is:

When we upload the code it is going to run through the setup code once. Control of the program goes down to the loop function. The call in the loop function is to the displayPattern function.

Control then goes to the displayPattern function. It uses all the variables it needs

to run it's code. The displayPattern function ends with a call to display(&currentPattern[0]).

That sends us to that function. Within that function, there is a call to the write74HC595(anodePins[i]) function. The program runs through that function then returns control back to display(unsigned int *anodePins)(The function call was display(&currentPattern[0]). It runs the one last line of code. Because that would be the end of the function with no further function call, control goes back to the loop function.

Back in the loop displayPattern(); is called again and it starts all over.

For beginners the most difficult part to this program could be the function calls and passing into functions..

Again I stress getting the first books in this series. They explain how to use serial monitor to see what your code is doing. It also explains if statements and for loops in detail.

The program is done. From here all the work is done in the anode pins array to make different patterns.

The sketch should now be:

****

```
// LedCube

// put your includes here

#include <Arduino.h>

// put your variables here
/* Shift Register variables */
int srClockPin=0;   // Pin connected to Pin 11 of 74HC595 (Clock SHCP)

int srLatchPin=1;   // Pin connected to Pin 12 of 74HC595 (Latch STCP)

int srDataPin=3;    // Pin connected to Pin 14 of 74HC595 (Data DS)

/* Cathode variables to be used in Cathode array */
int ledPin16= 4;

int ledPin17= 5;

int ledPin18= 6;

int ledPin19= 7;

// put your arrays here
int negativePins[] = {ledPin16, ledPin17, ledPin18, ledPin19};
unsigned char anodePins[] = {
// The shift register's outputs is connected to the anodes. There are 2 shift registers.
B00000000, B00000000, B00000000, B00000000, B00000000, B00000000, B00000000, B00000000,
};

// Put your supporting variables(attributes) here
int patternNumber=0;

int numPatterns=sizeof(anodePins)/8;
```

```
int tickCount=0;

int tickCountMax=50;

unsigned int currentPattern[4];

void setup()

{

        // put your setup code here, to run once:
        pinMode(srClockPin, OUTPUT);
        pinMode(srLatchPin, OUTPUT);
        pinMode(srDataPin, OUTPUT);

        // Setting cathodes to OUTPUT
        pinMode(ledPin16, OUTPUT);
        pinMode(ledPin17, OUTPUT);
        pinMode(ledPin18, OUTPUT);
        pinMode(ledPin19, OUTPUT);
}

// put your functions here

/* Shifting 8 bits of information per shift register into array */

void write74HC595(unsigned int hc595Value)

{

        digitalWrite(srLatchPin, LOW);
        shiftOut(srDataPin, srClockPin, LSBFIRST, hc595Value);
        shiftOut(srDataPin, srClockPin, LSBFIRST, (hc595Value >> 8));
        digitalWrite(srLatchPin, HIGH);
}

void display(unsigned int *anodePins)

{

        for (int i=0; i<4; i++)
        {
                for (int g=0; g<800; g++)
                {
                        if (g==0)
                        {
                                digitalWrite(negativePins[0], HIGH);
                                digitalWrite(negativePins[1], HIGH);
                                digitalWrite(negativePins[2], HIGH);
                                digitalWrite(negativePins[3], HIGH);
```

```
                        // Adding the values for the leds
                        write74HC595(anodePins[i]);
                        digitalWrite(negativePins[i], LOW);
                    }
                }
            }
        }

void displayPattern()

{

// only update it every tick otherwise just display as is

        tickCount--;
        if (tickCount <= 0)
        {
                tickCount = tickCountMax;
                for (int i=0; i<4; i++)
                {
                        currentPattern[i] = anodePins[i*2 + patternNumber*8] * 256 +
                        anodePins[i*2 + 1 + patternNumber*8];
                }
                patternNumber++;
                if (patternNumber >= numPatterns)
                {
                        patternNumber = 0;
                }
        }
        display(&currentPattern[0]);
}

void loop()

{

// put your main code here, to run repeatedly:

/* Adding function call to displayPattern() */

        displayPattern();

}
```

****

Verify then run your code. There should be no errors at this point.

The anodePins array now has to be explained. That is where you will be doing your code for

60

the patterns. It is safe to say that most of what you will be doing after this point is in the anodePins array.

CHAPTER 9: THE BITS AND BYTES OF IT

Create patterns to run on the cube in the anode array.

Going back to the anodePins array.

We will be using combinations of bits to light up a specific led.

There are 256 combinations available.

Don't worry it is going to be simple once you know the pattern.

Here is how it has been set up until now.

Just that is showing quite a bit about how it works.

Either shift register 1 or 2 will be used.

// Anode Array

```
unsigned char anodePins[] = {
// The shift register's outputs is connected to the anodes. There are 2 shift registers.
//   Shift      Shift      Shift      Shift      Shift      Shift      Shift      Shift
// Register   Register   Register   Register   Register   Register   Register   Register
//    1          2          1          2          1          2          1          2
B00000000, B00000000, B00000000, B00000000, B00000000, B00000000, B00000000, B00000000,
};
```

This is the creative part of the programming.

The micro-controller handles shifting the bits from the anode array into the shift register. Each shift register controls part of the cube. The leds will light up according to that process.

The name of the game is lighting the correct leds to make specific patterns on your cube, You have to change the correct anode to high. It is very important to know which serial register is controlling which anode.

That is the key to be able to easily make beautiful patterns on your cube.

It is more simple then you may think, and all it takes is the number 1 in the right spot.

Below is the elements in the anodePins array. These elements control the whole cube. They are the bits that will be shifted into the shift registers to turn them high or low.

B00000000, B00000000, B00000000, B00000000, B00000000, B00000000, B00000000, B00000000,

Depending on how you wire the cathodes will give your leds different results.

If you followed the layout of the cathodes for the assembly instructions earlier in this book, you will have.

The lowest level of the cube is the first section up from the shield. Let's say section one.

The next level up will be section 2. On to section three. The last level is section 4, the top section of the cube..

That means you have four sections of anodes which is D0 through D15

These are connected to the a cathode pin per section.

Section 4 – to D19.

Section 3 – to D18.

Section 2 – to D17.

Section 1 – to D16.

Each section has two sections depending on the shift register that controls it. Let's call them blocks.

Shift Register 1 controls D0 – D7 on all 4 sections. There are 8 leds on each block.

Shift Register 2 controls D8 – D15 on all 4 sections. There are 8 leds on each block.

Each block is 8 bits. That makes up a byte. Here we have 8 bytes in our array.

B00000000, B00000000, B00000000, B00000000, B00000000, B00000000, B00000000, B00000000,

The bits are all 0's or low, We are going to turn some to 1's or high and leave the rest low to start working with the cube.

For example if we want to light D0 Section 1:

B10000000, B00000000, B00000000, B00000000, B00000000, B00000000, B00000000, B00000000,

That was easy. But D0 is probably the easiest to figure out. Here you are counting through the blocks of bytes. D0 is the first byte of section 1.

So lets say we want to light up. D10 Section 3:

B00000000, B00000000, B00000000, B00000000, B00000000, B00100000, B00000000, B00000000,

This lights up that one led.

This led is a more difficult to figure out.

Each section is a level on the cube. The 3rd section is the third level from the bottom.

Now we have to figure out where that is on the array. We know each section has two sections or two bytes.

B00000000, B00000000, B00000000, B00000000, B00000000, B00000000, B00000000, B00000000,

The first section holds 2 bytes of bits.

B00000000 is a byte. The 00000000 is the bits. There are 8 0's meaning there are 8 bits. 8 bits make up a byte.

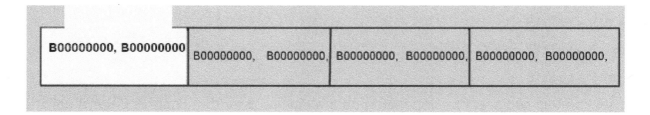

The first byte is for block D0 through D7. The second byte is for block D8 through D15. But this first section is for level one. So it is not what we want.

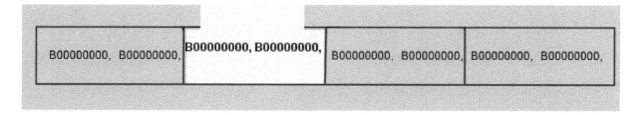

The next two bytes is for level 2 or section 2. Again this is not we we want.

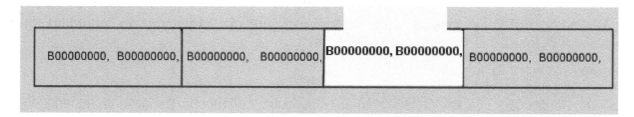

The next 2 bytes over. OK, this is level 3 or section 3. This is what we want.

B00000000, B00000000, NO	B00000000, B00000000, NO	B00000000, B00000000, YES	B00000000, B00000000, NO

Now we have to figure out which byte controls D10.

It will either be in the first byte or the second(Either shift register 1 or 2). So now count even though we know the first byte in this third block controls D0 through D7.

B	0	0	0	0	0	0	0	0
	1	2	3	4	5	6	7	8
	D0	D1	D2	D3	D4	D5	D6	D7

	Byte 1									Byte 2						
B	0	0	0	0	0	0	0	0	B	0	0	0	0	0	0	0	0
	1	2	3	4	5	6	7	8		1	2	3	4	5	6	7	8
	D0	D1	D2	D3	D4	D5	D6	D7		D8	D9	D10	D11	D12	D13	D14	D15

So it's like we thought the first byte is not what we are looking for.

When we count off the second byte we see that D10 is the third bit.

That brings us to our solution of :

B00000000, B00000000, B00000000, B00000000, B00000000, B00100000, B00000000, B00000000,

If we want to light them both:

B10000000, B00000000, B00000000, B00000000, B00000000, B00100000, B00000000, B00000000,

So you see it is a matter of changing 0(LOW) to 1(HIGH) where you want the led to light up.

That is the theory. Since we are not taught to think on a level of bits and bytes, it may take a moment to get the hang of it. But once you get the hang of it, you will be able to figure out where the bite should be 0 or 1 in a matter of seconds.

Are you beginning to see how it works?

If you think you do, try programming a square on your cube?

I got a fresh box of chocolate chip pecan cookies with my name on it. Just waiting to celebrate.

Try it and if you get lost come back to this point and we will go over it.

Think you got it??

Well, if your cube lit up correctly tells whether you have.

You should have only changed the bit code in the anodePins array.

To have a square. The code is below.

B11111001, B10011111, B11111001, B10011111, B11111001,B10011111, B11111001,B10011111,

Now that you got that under your hat. Let's try making an inside square.

When you get into it, you can think of many arrangements. Squares are the easiest.

There's x's and o's. Mini squares, half squares, etc.

This is a smaller cube so you are somewhat limited. But perfect to start you off.

The solution for the inside square is below.

B00000110, B01100000, B00000110, B01100000, B00000110, B01100000, B00000110, B01100000,

Now, if the flash is to fast you can slow it down by repeating the lines.

Below is some sample code, Take a look at it and run it.

Try to figure out how the lines work if you are still foggy on it.

Then try making some patterns of your own.

Remember all you are doing is adding these lines of code to the anodePins array.

When testing patterns you may find it useful to comment out lines you are not working on.

Here is the whole sketch below.

Example code courtesy of Ebonygeek45
****

```
// LedCube
// put your includes here
#include <Arduino.h>
```

```
// put your variables here
/* Shift Register variables */
int srClockPin=0;   // Pin connected to Pin 11 of 74HC595 (Clock SHCP)
int srLatchPin=1;   // Pin connected to Pin 12 of 74HC595 (Latch STCP)
int srDataPin=3;    // Pin connected to Pin 14 of 74HC595 (Data DS)
/* Cathode variables to be used in Cathode array */
int ledPin16= 4;
int ledPin17= 5;
int ledPin18= 6;
int ledPin19= 7;

// put your arrays here
int negativePins[] = {ledPin16, ledPin17, ledPin18, ledPin19};
// Anode Array
unsigned char anodePins[] = {
// The shift register's outputs is connected to the anodes. There are 2 shift registers.

B11111001,  B10011111,  B11111001,  B10011111,  B11111001,  B10011111,  B11111001,
B10011111,

B11111001,  B10011111,  B11111001,  B10011111,  B11111001,  B10011111,  B11111001,
B10011111,

B11111001,  B10011111,  B11111001,  B10011111,  B11111001,  B10011111,  B11111001,
B10011111,

B00000110, B01100000, B00000110, B01100000, B00000110, B01100000, B00000110, B01100000,

B00000110, B01100000, B00000110, B01100000, B00000110, B01100000, B00000110, B01100000,

B00000110, B01100000, B00000110, B01100000, B00000110, B01100000, B00000110, B01100000,

B11111001, B10011111, B11111001, B10011111, B00000000, B00000000, B00000000, B00000000,

B11111001, B10011111, B11111001, B10011111, B00000000, B00000000, B00000000, B00000000,

B11111001, B10011111, B11111001, B10011111, B00000000, B00000000, B00000000, B00000000,

B11111001, B10011111, B11111001, B10011111, B00000000, B00000000, B00000000, B00000000,

B11111001, B10011111, B11111001, B10011111, B00000000, B00000000, B00000000, B00000000,

B11111001, B10011111, B11111001, B10011111, B00000000, B00000000, B00000000, B00000000,

B00000000, B00000000, B00000000, B00000000, B11111001, B10011111, B11111001, B10011111,
```

```
B00000000, B00000000, B00000000, B00000000, B11111001, B10011111, B11111001, B10011111,
B00000000, B00000000, B00000000, B00000000, B11111001, B10011111, B11111001, B10011111,
B11111001, B10011111, B11111001, B10011111, B11111001, B10011111,  B11111001,B10011111,
B00000110, B01100000, B00000110, B01100000, B00000110, B01100000, B00000110, B01100000,
B11111001, B10011111, B11111001, B10011111, B00000000, B00000000, B00000000, B00000000,
B11111001, B10011111, B11111001, B10011111, B00000000, B00000000, B00000000, B00000000,
B00000000, B00000000, B00000000, B00000000, B11111001, B10011111, B11111001, B10011111,
};
// Put your supporting variables(attributes) here
int patternNumber=0;
int numPatterns=sizeof(anodePins)/8;
int tickCount=0;
int tickCountMax=50;
unsigned int currentPattern[4];

void setup()
{
        // put your setup code here, to run once:
        pinMode(srClockPin, OUTPUT);
        pinMode(srLatchPin, OUTPUT);
        pinMode(srDataPin, OUTPUT);

        // Setting cathodes to OUTPUT
        pinMode(ledPin16, OUTPUT);
        pinMode(ledPin17, OUTPUT);
        pinMode(ledPin18, OUTPUT);
        pinMode(ledPin19, OUTPUT);
}

// put your functions here
/* Shifting 8 bits of information per shift register into array */
void write74HC595(unsigned int hc595Value)
{
        digitalWrite(srLatchPin, LOW);
        shiftOut(srDataPin, srClockPin, LSBFIRST, hc595Value);
        shiftOut(srDataPin, srClockPin, LSBFIRST, (hc595Value >> 8));
```

```
        digitalWrite(srLatchPin, HIGH);
}
void display(unsigned int *anodePins)
{
        for (int i=0; i<4; i++)
        {
                for (int g=0; g<800; g++)
                {
                        if (g==0)
                        {
                                digitalWrite(negativePins[0], HIGH);
                                digitalWrite(negativePins[1], HIGH);
                                digitalWrite(negativePins[2], HIGH);
                                digitalWrite(negativePins[3], HIGH);
                                // Adding the values for the leds
                                write74HC595(anodePins[i]);
                                digitalWrite(negativePins[i], LOW);
                        }
                }
        }
}

/* Adding displayPattern() function. */
void displayPattern()
{
// only update it every tick otherwise just display as is
        tickCount--;
        if (tickCount <= 0)
        {
                tickCount = tickCountMax;
                for (int i=0; i<4; i++)
                {
                        currentPattern[i] = anodePins[i*2 + patternNumber*8] * 256 +
                        anodePins[i*2 + 1 + patternNumber*8];
                }
                patternNumber++;
                if (patternNumber >= numPatterns)
                {
                        patternNumber = 0;
                }
        }
```

```
        display(&currentPattern[0]);
}
void loop()
{
// put your main code here, to run repeatedly:
        displayPattern();

}
```

****

Have fun programming your cube.

CHAPTER 10: IN CLOSING

The Impulse is to just load the code to run it. Then find the part in the code that allows you to light the leds you want on the cube. It is strongly encouraged to actually study why the code is doing what it do. This book covers that. Understanding the code will help in future projects you do concerning shift registers. It will also help you in understanding coding in general. Especially arrays and passing arrays in functions.

Led cubes are beautiful. They are highly programmable. This particular kit can start you on your way. Then you can step up and make a bigger better one. That would give you the opportunity of creating your own circuit board for it. More than likely using wires diagram that you can create. Since you know a little more about it this may be a challenge, but it can be done. You have the skills to do it at this point..

Or you may want to make a cube that changes colors. This would involve RGB leds and more programming.

Maybe you have another type of project in mind. Like a reversed engineered car, or a small robot. This is something else that can benefit from a shift register or two or three.

Robotics is fun to get into. It may take more outputs then your micro-controller have. Shift Registers can do that for you. Here in this book it allows you to control 64 leds. That can be a major advantage for you in robotics. Robotics may require many servo's, dc motors, leds, sensors, speakers, more power, etc.

You now have experience working with IC's now. IC's can bring a whole new level to your programming. That is depending on which IC you decide to use, and there are many to choose from. They do a whole range of different things.

If you have a project in mind. There is an IC out there to help you complete it. Not to mention the IC's that you can get out of old toys to re-use in your projects.

There are also shields like the one used in this project. They are to take some of the headache out of all the wiring that would have to be done without it. For as many IC's as there are out there, there is also shields. I am fond of the prototyping shield that was used above to check the leds. It allows for quick prototyping of smaller projects without hooking up a lot more components to your breadboard.

Shields are just printed circuit boards. Using a multi-meter you can trace a shield and figure out what wiring you need if you want to create a project from scratch. As a matter of fact that is exactly what I did with this shield to make a diagram of what would be needed to do this cube without the shield.

A shield is just where someone did a prototype. Designed a diagram and had a pcb done off that design. Anyone can do that. The traces on the circuit board are just where the wiring would be. Some people do their on traces, so to speak on their perf boards. It depends on how "diy" you wan to be with your projects.

All in all keep prototyping, learning, building and coding. The more you do the better you will get at it. The more interesting things you will do.

The End.

Remember if you have an interesting pattern email it to ebonynerd45@gmail.com. We will try to get it up on YouTube.

There are other interesting sketches on the site;Ebonygeek Speak Arduino at:

https://sites.google.com/site/ebonygeekspeakarduino/

When you get there of course follow us on Facebook at:

https://www.facebook.com/Ebonygeek45-1248106408578282/

Follow us on Twitter at:

https://twitter.com/ebonygeek/

Subscribe to our YouTube Channel at:

https://www.youtube.com/Ebonygeek45

Order the Led 4x4x4 Cube kit for this project at:

http://www.icstation.com/icstation-4x4x4-light-cube-arduino-p-5312.html?aid=216

Click here if you would like to order the proto-board at:

http://www.icstation.com/prototype-shield-protoshield-mini-breadboard-arduino-duemila-p-2724.html?aid=216

For now happy building and happy coding.

Ebonygeek45

ABOUT THE AUTHOR

The ebonygeek45 brand is expanding. Continuing with the youtube videos and writing these books is a step up. It is enough to keep a person very busy. But the expansion is continuing. Plans are in the making for a small staff and better equipment for videos and photo's. Life is coming out sweet. It is truly amazing when you have a vision. Even if you only believe in that vision. Then to see it form right before your eyes. Truly amazing. Just a small update for you from ebonygeek45.